Up the Missouri River with Lewis and Clark

Up the Missouri River with Lewis and Clark

◆

From Camp Dubois to the Bad River

Bill Markley

iUniverse, Inc.

New York Lincoln Shanghai

Up the Missouri River with Lewis and Clark
From Camp Dubois to the Bad River

Copyright © 2005 by Bill Markley

iUniverse books may be ordered through booksellers or by contacting:

iUniverse
2021 Pine Lake Road, Suite 100
Lincoln, NE 68512
www.iuniverse.com
1-800-Authors (1-800-288-4677)

ISBN-13: 978-0-595-37272-0 (pbk)
ISBN-13: 978-0-595-81667-5 (ebk)
ISBN-10: 0-595-37272-4 (pbk)
ISBN-10: 0-595-81667-3 (ebk)

Printed in the United States of America

Dedicated to all those who seek reconciliation among all the peoples of the United States of America.

"We proceeded on."

Meriwether Lewis, William Clark, and the Corps of Discovery Sergeants used this phrase throughout their journals.

Contents

List of Illustrations

Foreword

Most of the books that have been written about the Lewis and Clark expedition—the Corps of Discovery, as they called themselves—discuss the trip from Montana onward to the Pacific. This segment might be more romantic than the earlier months of their adventure, the months where the captains were forced to punish some of their men in order to form a cohesive team that would obey orders without question. It's disturbing to hear about the courts martial of two privates who got drunk on the reserve supply of whiskey and were given lashes on their bare backs, or of a private who was forced to run the gauntlet for going AWOL. The captains were more compassionate in dealing with the private who went to sleep on duty, an infraction that could carry a death sentence. They administered 400 lashes instead, spread over four days.

It's easier to think of these men as dedicated adventurers, ready to follow orders from the start, placing themselves above human frailties. And it's much easier to think of the captains as benevolent and understanding, rather than strict masters who literally had to whip their men into shape.

The early part of the Corps' progress is also more burdensome to describe. Pulling a heavy keelboat against the current of the muddy Missouri is much less interesting than finding Sacajawea's long-lost Shoshone brother and borrowing horses to cross the mountains. Furthermore, crossing the Bitterroot Mountains was difficult, but it took only days. Pulling, rowing, and occasionally sailing up the Missouri took months. The sheer tedium keeps many writers from tackling this part of the expedition.

Bill Markley is not afraid to write about this part of the journey from the point of view of a resident of South Dakota and he does it well. We can suffer along with the men who get boils from the muddy river, men who become lost and are wary of Indians they have yet to meet. We read about stray animals that wander into camp, some kept, some not. We read about the death of Sergeant Floyd, who most writers dismiss as "amazingly, the only death on the expedition," and the subsequent silence and sadness of his grieving friends. The election of Patrick Gass to take Sergeant Floyd's place is described, as is the discovery of many new types of animals.

As the Corps travels westward, they encounter all types of weather as well as different tribes of Indians and their different attitudes toward the white men. All manner of insects plague them, the mosquitoes being especially troublesome. Clark complains about them constantly in his journal.

Read this account of the Corps of Discovery as they begin their two-year, four-month trip to the Pacific and you will get a better feel for the forming of a cohesive group. They would suffer many tribulations and share many conquests in the months and years ahead of them but it was their first months together that made them ready for the challenge.

Pat Decker Nipper
Author of *Love on the Lewis and Clark Trail*

Preface

The two hundredth anniversary of Lewis and Clark's Corps of Discovery expedition sparked a renewed interest in the expedition and the people, places, and things the Corps of Discovery encountered as it traveled from St. Louis to the Pacific Ocean and back. People have written volumes of material on the expedition, concentrating on its stay with the Mandan Tribe, Sacajawea, the Native American woman who greatly aided the expedition, the Nez Pierce Tribe who offered friendship and horses, the expedition's struggle through the Bitterroot Mountains, first sighting of the Pacific Ocean, and its winter over in the Northwest. Authors tend to rush through the first leg of the journey as the members of the Corps of Discovery learn about each other and the country they pass through; but it is during the first four months of the expedition up the Missouri River that the men forge themselves into a team that Clark calls his Band of Brothers.

In the spring of 2004, I approached Don Boyd, editor of the *River Life* newspaper, with an idea for a series of articles on Lewis and Clark's expedition. The series would cover the expedition from Camp Dubois, its Illinois base camp, to the Pierre and Fort Pierre area in South Dakota where the Corps had its first encounter with the Brule Tribe of the Lakota people or as Lewis and Clark called them the Teton Sioux. My premise was to provide biweekly installments chronicling the expedition as it headed up the Missouri River and approached Pierre and Fort Pierre. Don was intrigued and gave me the assignment. As the seven part series progressed, readers enjoyed following along with the Corps of Discovery's exploits.

This book is a compilation of those seven articles. I used the journals kept by Meriwether Lewis, William Clark, the Sergeants Patrick Gass, Charles Floyd, John Ordway, and Private Joseph Whitehouse. Professor Gary Moulton's edited version of their journals with his extensive footnotes and appendices were invaluable in providing insight into the men of the expedition and their backgrounds. I used several secondary sources to get an overall feel for the Corps of Discovery and its members. For the most part, I relied on the participants' actual journals. In some cases, I use the exact quotes from the journals including their spelling. I like their free and random spelling; it makes my spelling look good. We have to remember that Americans did not have standardized spelling in 1804–1806. Noah Webster published his first preliminary dictionary in 1806, and spell check did not come about until the late 20th Century.

The front cover photograph and all illustrations are used with permission of the South Dakota Office of Tourism. Special thanks to Chad Coppess, Senior Photographer with the South Dakota Office of Tourism, who took the photographs, provided support and expert advice as to what illustrations to use, and put them in a format for this publication. Most of the photographs are of the modern-day reenactment group, The Discovery Expedition of St. Charles, Missouri. The following is their mission statement:

> The Discovery Expedition of St. Charles, Missouri, is a nonprofit organization dedicated to rediscovering the legacy of Lewis and Clark. Each year the Discovery Expedition reenacts a portion of the original river journey, from Elizabeth, Pennsylvania, where the keelboat was built in 1803, to Great Falls, Montana, beyond which the original boats could not proceed. We are official reenactors for the waterway portion of the national Lewis and Clark bicentennial commemoration.

The Discovery Expedition of St. Charles, Missouri passed through South Dakota during the summer of 2004. Chad took the photographs of them as they progressed up the Missouri River.

Alex Rodriguez, GIS consultant for Factor 360, with advice from Ron Woodburn, Director of Capital University Center created the maps of the Corps of Discovery's journey from Camp Dubois, Illinois to the Bad River, South Dakota. The map's black dots represent modern cities; and the black triangles represent some of the Corps of Discovery's significant events and stops along the way. The modern boundaries of the states are displayed to help orient the map reader.

Lewis and Clark's Corps of Discovery caused eventual changes in the lands and the people it encountered as it passed through on its way to the Pacific Ocean and back. As in any experience or trip, there are good and bad outcomes as well as more than one point of view. I wrote this book from the point of view of the men of the Corps of Discovery who kept a written record of what they did and observed. So without further discussion and in the words of the men of the Corps of Discovery, let us proceed on.

Acknowledgements

Don Boyd, thank you for publishing in *River Life* my "Up The River" series of articles that form the basis for this book. Without Gary Moulton's *The Definitive Journals of Lewis and Clark*, this book would not be in the format that it is. Thanks to my wife, Liz, for her manuscript reviews and patience with me. Thanks to my children, Chris and Becky, for your support. Thanks to the South Dakota Office of Tourism and especially Chad Coppess for your wonderful artwork for the cover and illustrations. Thanks to Alex Rodriguez for creating the maps, and thanks to Ron Woodburn for his map advice. Thanks to Pat Nipper, author of *Love on the Lewis and Clark Trail*, for your support and review. Thank you to Bill Stevens, President of Encounters on the Prairie, Central South Dakota Chapter of the Lewis and Clark Trail Heritage Foundation, for your support. Lenore Puhek, Bill Aisenbrey, Julie Linn, and Sheryl Torguson thanks for your editorial critiques. Mike Fiedler and Joyce Greenfield with iUniverse.com thank you for your assistance and help with the production of this book. Thanks to my mom, Gloria Markley, and brother, Doug, and his family for all your support. Finally, I thank the Lord for my life and the experiences placed before me.

Introduction—If It Wasn't For Haiti

The Caribbean nation of Haiti was recently in the news with revolution, deposing of the president, and intervention of United States troops to restore order. But did you know that if it wasn't for Haiti, western states such as South Dakota might not be here. "How so?" you might ask.

To find out why, we need to step back in time to the 1700's and look at the thirteen British Colonies that would become the United States and also look at the Louisiana Territory. France originally settled and controlled Louisiana. During most of the 1700's, France and Great Britain fought a series of wars against each other. Americans called them the French and Indian Wars. Great Britain finally won in 1762 taking control of Canada with Spain taking control of Louisiana.

American colonists began to cross the Appalachian Mountains into territory that would become the states of Ohio, Kentucky, and Tennessee. During the Revolutionary War, the settlers west of the Appalachian Mountains shipped their produce down the Mississippi to New Orleans for export. The Spanish allowed this because during the Revolution they sided with the Americans against the British. After the war, the Spanish refused American frontier settlers the use of the port of New Orleans. Why was this a concern to Americans? It was a lot easier and cheaper to ship produce down the river than to have to transport the produce over the mountains to the east coast states. After years of negotiations, the Spanish once again allowed Americans the use of the port of New Orleans.

In 1789, the French Revolution began. People of French heritage in Louisiana hoped that they would again become a part of France. Spain wanted to keep Louisiana as a buffer between their Mexican gold mines and the Americans. America wanted to keep exporting its produce through the port of New Orleans.

This brings us to Haiti. Haiti is the western mountainous part of the island of Hispaniola. Pirates controlled the western portion of the island and the Spanish the eastern portion. France eventually subdued the pirates, took control of the western half of the island, and brought in Africans to work as slaves on sugar plantations. Sugar from Haiti was a major part of the French economy. In 1791, the slaves revolted against their French masters and won their freedom. This further worsened the French economy.

In 1799, Napoleon Bonaparte seized power in France. He wanted to revitalize the French economy by reestablishing Haiti as a colony and reinstalling the Haitians as slaves. To support the Haitian slave economy, Napoleon needed Louisiana as a base to supply food and material to Haiti. In 1800, he signed a secret treaty with Spain returning Louisiana to France. At this point, the Spanish authorities in New Orleans closed the port to Americans disrupting the American frontier economy again.

In 1802, Napoleon sent 15,000 troops to Haiti to reinstall slavery. But between Haitian freedom fighters and yellow fever carried by mosquitoes, the French were defeated.

During this time, President Thomas Jefferson had instructed Robert Livingston, his special envoy to France, to try to buy New Orleans so American frontier farmers could resume produce shipments. Napoleon refused until he realized he could not control Haiti. When Napoleon determined his troops could not hold Haiti, he had no need for Louisiana.

Napoleon instructed his negotiators to tell the Americans they could not only buy New Orleans but all of Louisiana—almost 900,000 square miles for fifteen million dollars. In 1803, the United States bought the Louisiana Territory and as they say, the rest is history.

The year 2004 marked the 200th anniversary of Lewis and Clark's Corps of Discovery heading up the Missouri River to see what the United States had bought. As you can see, South Dakota and other western states, in part, owe their existence to rebel Haitian slaves. Otherwise, I might say to you in closing "Au revoir!"

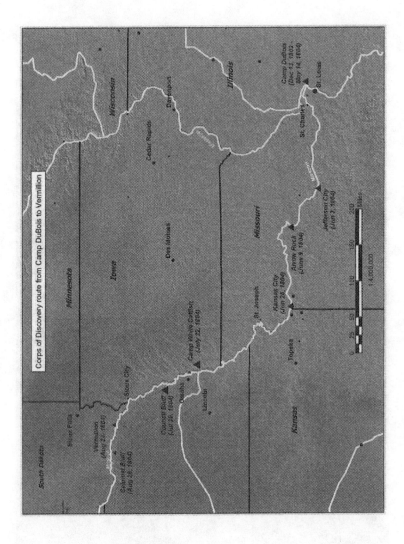

Corps of Discovery route from Camp DuBois to Vermillion

1

May 14–June 26, 1804

Rain fell from the overcast sky. Enough breeze came from out of the northeast to fill the sail and propel the keelboat westward. The men on board were in high spirits even though it was not the best weather to start a cross-continent trip. So began one of the great American adventures.

At 4:00 p.m., on May 14, 1804, after more than a year of preparation, the United States Corps of Discovery set out from Camp Dubois, its winter camp on the Illinois bank of the Mississippi River. The 55-foot keelboat, loaded down with food, supplies, and gifts for Indian tribes, and two smaller boats, called pirogues, crossed the Mississippi River to the mouth of the Missouri River and headed upriver four miles.

President Thomas Jefferson appointed his personal secretary, thirty-year-old Meriwether Lewis, to lead the expedition and Lewis chose his friend, thirty-four-year-old William Clark to be his co-leader. Both men were in the military and had had previous dealings with Indian tribes.

The Corps of Discovery was a military expedition so Lewis and Clark would enforce military discipline. The men were armed with Pennsylvania long rifles some of which were the first issues from the new United States arsenal at Harpers Ferry, Virginia. Lewis and Clark had a small brass cannon mounted on a swivel at the bow of the keelboat. They had two blunderbusses mounted on swivels at the keelboat's stern and a blunderbuss mounted at the bow of each pirogue. The Corps started out with approximately 42 men. Most of these men had experience in backwoods living. The number of people associated with the Corps of Discovery would fluctuate over the course of the expedition.

President Jefferson said the Corps of Discovery's mission was to proceed up the Missouri River to its source and then find a passage to the

Pacific Ocean. They were to come in peace to the local inhabitants and inform them that they were now part of the United States. Lewis and Clark were to determine the prospects for trade, and take notes on local peoples and their customs. They were to take scientific observations and record their encounters.

In 1803, the United States had bought the Louisiana Territory from France in a secret treaty, after Spain had secretly returned Louisiana to France. Confusing? Even though he knew about the secret deals between Spain and France, and France and the United States, the Spanish official in St. Louis would not allow the Corps of Discovery to be based in Louisiana Territory, the west bank of the Mississippi, until the territory was officially transferred on March 9, 1804.

On May 14, while William Clark led the expedition up the Missouri, Meriwether Lewis was still in St. Louis finishing administrative details for the expedition and arranging for American Indian leaders to go to Washington to meet with President Jefferson. While in St. Louis, Meriwether stayed with his new friends the Chouteau brothers, Pierre and Auguste. The Chouteau brothers were influential St. Louis businessmen who helped outfit the Corps of Discovery. (As a note, Pierre and Fort Pierre, South Dakota, are named for Pierre Chouteau's son.)

May 16, twenty-two-year-old Sergeant Charles Floyd from Kentucky wrote, "arrived at St. Charles at 2 o'clock Pm one gun fired a Grait nomber of Friench people Came to see the Boat." French pioneers settled St. Charles in 1769 and at this time, 450 people lived there. The men spent their time reloading the keelboat and socializing with the citizens as they waited for Lewis to join them. During a rainstorm on May 20, Lewis and a number of St. Louis friends including Auguste Chouteau arrived in St. Charles by horseback. The next day, May 21, with a shout of three cheers from friends and townspeople, the Corps of Discovery left St. Charles heading west, upriver.

The expedition passed Boone's Settlement on May 23. Daniel Boone had started the settlement and currently lived there. Did Lewis and Clark meet him? They left no record if they did. Maybe old Daniel was out hunting.

Meriwether Lewis climbed Tavern Rocks to see Tavern Cave and its pictographs at the top of the cliffs. His participation in the expedition could have ended here. He slipped over the side and was able to save himself from a three hundred foot drop by stabbing his knife into the side of the steep descent coming to a stop twenty feet down.

May 25, the Corps of Discovery passed the village of La Charette consisting of five families, the last white settlement on the Missouri River. The residents of La Charette gave the men of the expedition milk and eggs.

On June 1, the Corps of Discovery reached the Osage River, which is about the midpoint of the Missouri River as it flows through today's state of Missouri.

The evening of June 3, the Corps of Discovery camped at the mouth of the Moreau River, just downriver of present-day Jefferson City, capital of Missouri. It had been a cloudy rainy day. Clark wrote that he saw where Indians had crossed the river and "I have a verry Sore Throat, (great) & am Tormented with Musquetors & Small ticks."

The river current was against them at about five miles an hour. They had to be careful of whirlpools, swift currents, shifting sandbars, and floating trees on and below the surface of the river. Some of these trees called sawyers were imbedded into the river bottom. The Corps of Discovery needed to be careful of overhanging tree limbs. William Clark wrote on June 4, "the Sergt. at the helm run under a bending Tree & broke the mast."

After a hard rain on the night of June 8, the Corps of Discovery set out early the next day. The current was "exceedingly strong," according to Clark.

They were just past the present-day town of Arrow Rock, Missouri, when a submerged log snagged the keelboat's stern. The current swung the bow of the boat downstream so now the keelboat was broadside to the river's flow. The boat smashed into submerged trees that held it against the strong current. Clark wrote, "This was a disagreeable and Dangerous Situation, particularly as immense large trees were Drifting down and we lay immediately in their Course." Some of the men grabbed the keelboat's rope, jumped over the side into the swift current, swam to shore where they braced themselves, and pulled the keelboat off the snag. That evening, Clark wrote in his journal, "I can Say with Confidence that our party is not inferior to any that was ever on the waters of the Missoppie."

The expedition started out with two horses to use for hunting. The number of horses changed during the course of the expedition. Hunters would set out each day and bring back game to add to the food supply. Charles Floyd wrote on June 11, "ouer hunters Kiled 2 Bar & 2 Deer."

June 12, they met two pirogues coming downriver loaded with pelts. The leader of the group was Pierre Dorion, Sr., a family friend of the Clarks back in Illinois. Pierre was married to a woman who was a member of the Yankton Sioux Tribe and he had been living with the tribe. William persuaded the old family friend to join them to act as interpreter and introduce them to the Yanktons.

The men came down with boils and dysentery. Clark blamed the river water and told the men to make sure they dipped well below the surface scum when fetching water.

Clark had been off hunting by himself. On Sunday, June 24, he wrote, "I joined the Boat theis morning with a fat Bear & two Deer. Last evening…I concluded to camp although I had nothing but my hunting Dress, & Musquitors Ticks & Knats very troublesome." During this day, the men saw immense herds of deer and plenty of bear sign.

By June 26, the Corps of Discovery had traveled 400 miles to where the Missouri River makes a sharp bend from the west to the north.

2

June 26–July 8, 1804

The Corps of Discovery had reached the mouth of the Kansas River across from present-day Kansas City, Missouri, on June 26, 1804. They decided to camp there until June 29, and then continue up the Missouri River. The men built a brush wall for protection and set up tents within the structure. They spent their time repairing equipment, rearranging cargo, hunting, and exploring. Some of the hunters had seen herds of buffalo to the west.

Privates Reubin and Joseph Fields were brothers who were part of the original group of nine men William Clark brought with him from Kentucky. They were expert shots and were usually out hunting for game. While out on a hunt, they killed a wolf and captured a second young wolf to keep as a pet. No one wrote if Seaman, Meriwether Lewis' Newfoundland dog, got along with the wolf.

Lewis had bought Seaman for twenty dollars sometime before the beginning of the expedition. In 1803, Seaman traveled with Lewis down the Ohio River from Pittsburgh, Pennsylvania, on the newly constructed keelboat. Seaman was an enthusiastic hunter. On September 11, 1803, Lewis wrote, "...observed a number of squirrels swimming the Ohio and universally passing from the W. to the East shore they appear to be making to the south...I made my dog take as many each day as I had occation for, they are fat and I thought them when fried a pleasant food...my dog...would take the squirrel in the water kill them and swimming bring them in his mouth to the boat."

During the night of June 28, 1804, Private John Collins was on duty guarding the whiskey barrels, which the men were storing on shore for the evening. Whiskey was one of the few luxury items the men had with them.

The whiskey would not last the entire trip and there was no place to get more. They had been rationing the whiskey so it would last longer. Once a day, Lewis and Clark allowed each man one gill of whiskey. A gill is a fourth of a pint.

Sometime during the night, John Collins' good friend and partner in crime, Private Hugh Hall, joined him at the whiskey barrels while the rest of the men slept. One of them got the bright idea to sample the whiskey. After all what could a few sips hurt?

John and Hugh had been in trouble before. Back in Illinois during the Corps of Discovery's winter camp, John had stolen a farmer's pig. John and Hugh had both been in trouble in St. Charles for being absent without leave from the boat; John had additional charges of behaving in an unbecoming manner at a ball, and speaking in a language that disrespected the commanding officer's orders. The Corps of Discovery held a court-martial letting Hugh off but giving John fifty lashes. John would not be the kind of person to give the responsibility of guarding the whiskey.

John and Hugh proceeded to have more than a few sips and by morning they were drunk. A court-martial convened. Sergeant Nathaniel Hale Pryor presided. John pleaded not guilty and was sentenced "to recive one hundred Lashes on his bear Back." Hugh pleaded guilty and the court sentenced him to receive fifty lashes on his bare back. Lewis and Clark approved the sentences of the court and the men carried out the sentences later that day. The Corps of Discovery then packed their remaining gear into the boats, proceeded up river at 4 p.m., and made camp late in the evening.

On June 30, William Clark wrote "Deer to be Seen in every direction and their tracks ar as plenty as Hogs about a farm." They again broke their mast on an overhanging tree as they pulled into shore. That night a sentry challenged "either a man or Beast, which run off, all prepared for action," Clark wrote. The men were in good health except for their boils.

It was hard rowing against the current. On July 1, the men were tired from the heat and their exertion. Lewis and Clark gave them a three-hour break. July 2, the current was so strong against the keelboat that Clark wrote "we could with dificuelty Stem the Current with our 20 oars & and all the poles we had."

July 3, the men found and kept a tame, well-fed, white horse.

The morning of July 4, the Corps of Discovery fired the swivel cannon to commemorate Independence Day; and they fired it again in the evening. This was the first Fourth of July celebration west of the Mississippi River. Lewis and Clark gave the men an extra gill of whiskey to celebrate.

One incident marred the festive day; a snake bit Joe Fields on the side of his foot, which swelled up. Lewis applied a poultice to the wound to draw out the poison. Later they passed an extensive prairie that Clark named Jo Fields Snake Prairie. They had earlier passed a creek and named it Independence Creek. Sergeant Charles Floyd described their evening camp in his journal, "we camped at one of the Butifules Praries I ever Saw open and butifully Divided with Hills and vallies all presenting themselves."

Sergeant John Ordway wrote on Thursday, July 5, "we passed Some verry bad Sand bars the Boat turned three times once on a Drift wood, but recived no procevable Damage, we came too at a beaver house for Dinner." Lewis' dog, Seaman, entered the beaver hut and drove out the hut's residents.

A whippoorwill, a small nocturnal bird, perched on the keelboat during the daytime on July 6. Those who are superstitious associate seeing a whippoorwill and hearing its call with death. Most of the men recorded the incident in their journals.

The day was so hot that Clark wrote, "Those men that do not work at all will wet a Shirt in a Few minits & those who work, the Swet will run off in Streams."

Patrick Gass, an Irishman from Pennsylvania, wrote that they killed a wolf and a large wood rat on July 7. Private Robert Frazer came down with heat exhaustion; but Lewis bled him and gave him niter, which "revived him much." Niter is potassium nitrate also known as saltpeter. Lewis had received medical training in Philadelphia from Dr. Benjamin Rush who was one of the top physicians in the country.

At 7:00 p.m., an intense thunder and lightning storm hit for a half hour accompanied by high winds, rain, and a drop in the river's water level.

On July 8, five of the men developed "violent" headaches. Lewis and Clark signed an order dividing the men into three messes to better distribute the food and provide a more orderly way of food preparation and eating. The hunters continued to find plenty of game to add to their menu. The Corps of Discovery was now north of present-day St. Joseph, Missouri.

3

July 9–22, 1804

By July 9, 1804, the Corps of Discovery had traveled on the Missouri River to a position upriver from present-day St. Joseph, Missouri. One of their objectives was to inform the tribes who lived along the river that they were now part of the United States and that the Corps of Discovery came in peace and friendship. They had yet to see, let alone meet any tribes. The French engagés, or workers, told Lewis and Clark the tribes were probably off hunting buffalo at this time of year.

The Corps of Discovery traveled twelve miles upriver before setting up camp for the night. Several of the men were hunting on the far side of the river and did not plan to return that evening. The Corps saw a fire on the far shore. Thinking it was the hunters, they sent a pirogue over to let the hunters know they were across the river. When the men in the pirogue paddled near the fire on the riverbank, they shouted to who they thought were the hunters. It appeared someone immediately put out the fire; and no one responded to their shouts. The men in the pirogue reported to Lewis and Clark what had happened. Thinking it could be a Sioux war party, Lewis and Clark had the swivel cannon fired to warn the hunters. That night they were ready to repel any attacks.

The next day, they went to the site of last night's fire on the far bank to discover it was their hunters after all. The hunters had gone to sleep early. Due to the direction of the wind, they never heard the shouts or the swivel cannon. The Corps of Discovery made another ten miles that day.

July 11, 1804, while out exploring on his own, Clark found another stray horse. They made six miles that day and camped on a sand island opposite the Big Nemaha River just above the present Nebraska-Kansas

State line. Sergeant Charles Floyd wrote, "Came to about 12 oclock P.m. for the porpos of resting one or two days the men is all Sick"

That evening Private Alexander Hamilton Willard was on sentry duty. Alexander was born in New Hampshire in 1778. He had moved to Kentucky, had training as a blacksmith, and had been a member of Captain Amos Stoddard's artillery company that took possession of St. Louis for the United States.

The men were tired and sick. They would be spending a day or two on this island to recuperate. Alexander must have been exhausted. Why not lay down for a minute? Why not close the eyes just for a second?

Next morning the first thing Alexander knew, Sergeant John Ordway was accusing him of lying down and sleeping at his post. Alexander admitted he was lying down, but not sleeping.

Lewis and Clark had to convene and preside over this court-martial instead of the men since the guilty sentence could mean death. They determined Alexander was asleep at his post. What to do? They needed every man; but they could not lose discipline. They decided on a middle course of action; 400 lashes on Alexander Willard's bare back, one hundred each evening at sunset.

That day Clark took a few men in a pirogue up the Big Nemaha River to explore. They found numerous large artificial mounds built by people many years ago; and it appeared people were still using these highpoints for burial practices.

July 13, 1804, the Corps of Discovery made over twenty miles this day and stopped at a large sandbar in the middle of the river for the night.

The next morning, it was raining hard when they set off and began passing the rest of the sandbar. The riverbanks were sloughing into the current. Just as they passed the end of the sand island, the rainstorm intensified. A sudden squall hit the keelboat forcing it back onto the sandbar. All the men jumped off into the water to hold the boat off the bar. Some of the men were able to manhandle the cable and anchor out into the river to assist in keeping the boat from wrecking on the island. The storm lasted forty minutes. Clark was sure that their efforts kept the boat from "being thrown up on the Sand Island, and dashed to pieces." The storm abated and the surface of the river was as smooth as glass.

Everything was in good shape except for Clark's notes, "My notes of the 13th of July by a Most unfortunate accident blew over Board in a Storm…obliges me to refur to the Journals of Serjeants, and my own recollection."

The Corps continued upriver. Clark and George Drouillard were walking on shore when they saw three elk at the water's edge and shot at them. The elk were too far off to hit. Seaman saw the elk run, jumped out of the boat, and swam after them, but could not catch up with them. The Corps made nine miles upriver this day.

Thick fog prevented the men from starting out as early as they had wanted to on the morning of July 15. They made over nine miles and encamped on a woody point. Clark had been off exploring alone again. While waiting for the boat to catch up, he swam across the mouth of the Little Nemaha River and hiked three miles further upriver to wait for the rest of the expedition.

Meanwhile, Lewis was keeping scientific records. Compared to Clark and the Sergeants' accounts, Lewis' journal entries are dry. He makes distance, time, and weather observations. On this day, he was having problems with one of his instruments and writes, "This evening I discovered that my Chronometer had stoped, nor can I assign any cause for this accident: she had been wound up the preceding noon as usual. This is the third instance in which this instrument has stopt in a similar manner since she has been in my possession…"

Sergeant Charles Floyd writes on July 16, "we Set out verry early and prossed on the Side of a Prarie the wind from the South Sailed ouer Boat Run on a Sawyer Sailed all day made 20 miles passed Sevrall Isd Camt on the North Side."

The Corps decided to stay at this campsite for the day on July 17 to make some corrections to the scientific equipment and allow the men to rest. Several of them still had boils. Later that day Lewis joined the hunters who killed four deer.

July 18, the Corps passed large islands, a long hillside that had slumping into the river leaving a steep bluff, and treacherous sandbars. The men found a starving, stray dog, fed him meat, and tried to coax the dog to following them; but he would not join them.

The next morning after a breakfast of deer ribs and coffee, Clark set out alone while the Corps continued upstream. "Soon after I got on Shore, Saw Some fresh elk Sign, which I was induced to prosue those animals by their track to the hills after assending and passing thro a narrow Strip of wood Land, Came Suddenly into an open and bound less Prarie, I say bound less because I could not See the extent of the plain in any Derection…This prospect was So Sudden & entertaining that I forgot the object of my prosute…"

On July 20, the Corps traveled eighteen miles before camping for the night. While out hunting, Clark killed "an emence large yellow wolf."

After 600 miles and 68 days, the Corps of Discovery reached the mouth of the Platte River on July 21. Beyond this point, few white traders had ventured; the land would be changing to predominately prairie; and this was the beginning of Sioux territory.

Lewis and Clark ascended the Platte River in a Pirogue for a mile taking scientific observations. The Corps worked its way around the sandbars at the mouth of the Platte and camped that night along the Missouri River upstream of the Platte's mouth. The men saw and heard a large number of wolves that evening.

July 22, 1804, the Corps of Discovery continued up the Missouri River ten miles and set up camp for a few days. Lewis and Clark decided they would send out scouts to find the local tribes and invite them to their camp so they could, "…let them know of the Change of Government, The wishes of our Government to Cultivate friendship with them, the Objects of our journey and to present them with a flag and Some Small presents."

4

July 23–August 5, 1804

Camp White Catfish, Monday, July 23, 1804. The Corps of Discovery had traveled ten miles upriver of the Platte River and set up camp on the east bank of the Missouri River. They planned to stay at this camp several days hoping to make contact with the Oto and Pawnee Tribes. Meriwether Lewis and William Clark sent Pierre Cruzatte and George Drouillard to find the tribes and invite them to Camp White Catfish for a meeting. Cruzatte had been in the area before and knew there was an Oto town eighteen miles up the Platte River with a Pawnee town further beyond that.

Private Pierre Cruzatte enlisted as an interpreter with the Corps of Discovery at St. Charles on May 16, 1804. Cruzatte was half-French and half-Omaha. He had lost one eye and he was nearsighted in the remaining eye. Pierre was a good fiddle player and entertained the men with his music.

George Drouillard was the son of a French-Canadian father and a Shawnee mother. He had met Lewis in November 1803, and agreed to serve as an interpreter. He was good at sign language and along with the Field brothers, he was one of the Corps best hunters.

The Corps of Discovery spent its time improving the camp, hunting, drying out gear and supplies, and making new paddles, oars, and poles.

The wind blew hard out of the south on July 24. Private Silas Goodrich, considered one of the Corps best fishermen, caught a white catfish that may have been a channel catfish. The hunters killed two deer and a turkey.

Cruzatte and Drouillard returned to camp on July 25, they had traveled as far as the Oto town; but did not find anyone. The Otos were off hunting buffalo. The Corps hunters again killed two deer and a turkey.

July 26, the wind was again blowing out of the south. Clark wrote that the winds blew clouds of sand so hard that he could not write in his tent or on the boat. He retreated to the woods where he was out of the wind, but had "Combat with Musquitors." The men caught and ate five beaver. One of the men had a very large boil on his chest. Clark lanced the boil, which discharged a half pint of fluid.

At 1:30 p.m. on July 27, the Corps of Discovery set out again on its upriver journey sailing with a gentle breeze. After making camp, Clark and Rubin Field went on a walk to examine manmade mounds that covered over two hundred acres. While on their walk, they killed a deer. Clark wrote the "Misquiters" were the size of houseflies and raged all night.

The next morning was "Dark Smokey" and raining as the Corps continued upriver. While out hunting, Drouillard found three elk hunters who belonged to the Missouri Tribe. They gave Drouillard some elk meat and told him they lived with the Otos. One of the hunters agreed to return to camp with Drouillard. The man said he belonged to a camp of twenty lodges located four miles away. Beyond that camp was a larger group who had a French trader living with them.

Private Joseph Whitehouse wrote, "we...proceeded on one Mile, when the boat struck a sand barr, on her larbourd Side, and all hands were obliged to jump out in the Water to prevent her from sinking."

The Corps traveled twelve miles upriver before making camp for the night.

On July 29, Lewis and Clark sent the Missouri man back to his band with La Liberté, a French engagé. Lewis and Clark instructed La Liberté who was fluent in Oto to invite the Missouris and Otos to the Corps' camp that would be located further upriver.

The Corps passed through an area that a tornado must have devastated. Trees, some with trunk diameters of four feet, had been snapped off near the ground.

The next morning, the men discovered the white horse that Clark had found had died during the night. The Corps continued upstream and camped about fifteen miles north of present day Omaha, Nebraska. They would wait here for the Otos and Missouris to join them. The men set up a flagpole, hoisted the American flag, and called the place Camp Badger, but later changed the name to Council Bluffs Camp.

The reason they at first called it Camp Badger was that Joe Field had killed an eighteen-pound badger. This was the first one most of the men had seen. Everyone who kept a journal described it in great detail. They skinned and stuffed the badger to send back to President Jefferson.

Sergeant Charles Floyd wrote, "I am verry Sick and Has ben for Some-time but have Recoverd my helth again."

The men caught catfish and killed geese and turkeys. They cleaned and inspected their weapons, and even though they were still coming down with boils, they were in high spirits. Joe and Rubin Field rode off hunting again, but did not return that night.

On July 31, the Field brothers returned—on foot. They had killed three deer; but the horses had wandered off. Lewis and Clark sent men out to find the horses, but with no luck. George Drouillard caught a small, tame beaver and kept it for a pet.

The next day, Lewis and Clark sent Drouillard and Private John Colter to find the horses. They sent Private George Gibson back to Camp White Catfish to look for the Otos, Missouris, and La Liberté. Gibson found no sign that anyone had been to the camp.

At the end of the day, Clark wrote, "The Indians not yet arrived we fear Something amiss with our Messinger or them."

Drouillard and Colter returned on August 2, with the horses and an elk they had shot. They found the horses twelve miles south of the Corps' camp. At sunset, six Oto and Missouri chiefs and their warriors arrived at the camp along with the French trader, Faufon.

Clark wrote, "...Capt. Lewis & myself met those Indians & informed them we were glad to See them, and would Speak to them tomorrow, Sent them Som rosted meat Pork flour & meal, in return they Sent us Water millions [watermelons]."

Even though the Otos and Missouris appeared friendly, Lewis and Clark set out a strong guard for the night.

August 3, the men set up the mainsail as an awning for the meeting. The chiefs, warriors, and Faufon arrived in camp. The sergeants paraded the soldiers. Lewis gave a long speech about coming in friendship and about the change of government to the United States. Lewis and Clark gave the chiefs presents including peace medals that had the likeness of President Jefferson. They smoked. The chiefs asked for a little whiskey, powder and ball which Lewis and Clark gave them. The Otos and Missouris gave the Corps more watermelons. The chiefs told Lewis and Clark that the major chiefs of the Otos, Little Thief and Big Horse, were out hunting buffalo. Each chief gave a speech stating he was pleased with the change in government.

Lewis and Clark asked about La Liberté. The chiefs said he had been to their town and had left a day before they had. Clark was concerned La Liberté's horse had given out or that he was lost on the plains. The Otos and Missouris said they would search for him. Lewis fired his novelty air gun for their entertainment. The Corps then bid goodbye to the Otos and Missouris, set sail, and made camp five miles further upriver. Private Moses Reed had left his knife behind at the Council Bluffs Camp and asked for permission to go back and get it. He was told he could go ahead and do that.

After an early morning storm on August 4, the Corps continued upriver. They passed through a mile stretch of river where the current was undercutting the bank, and trees were falling into the river. They passed a deserted trading house where Pierre Cruzatte and others had spent two years trading with the local tribes. By nightfall, Reed had not caught up with the Corps.

August 5, the morning started out with a strong wind from the northeast, clouds, and rain. The men killed a large bull snake that was after some little birds; and Lewis killed two least terns that he described in his journal in great detail.

As they made camp that night, La Liberté and Moses Reed were still missing. Everyone was concerned for their safety. Had they run into trouble or had they deserted?

5

August 6–19, 1804

It was August 6, 1804. The Corps of Discovery had traveled up the Missouri River beyond present-day Omaha, Nebraska. A few days before, they had met with chiefs of the Oto and Missouri Tribes. On a negative note, two members of the Corps were now missing.

A violent storm had hit the campsite at midnight. That morning the Corps of Discovery "Set out early & proceeded on." They made over twenty miles on this day. Lewis and Clark believed the French engage, La Liberté, had become lost; but they were beginning to suspect Moses Reed had deserted. He had asked to go back to Council Bluffs to retrieve a knife and should have caught up with the Corps by now.

Again, there was another violent windstorm during the night. William Clark wrote, "mosquitors more troublesome last night than I ever Saw them."

At 1:00 p.m., Lewis and Clark sent George Drouillard, Rubin Field, William Bratton, and Francois Labiche to find, La Liberté and Reed. They were ordered if Reed "did not give up Peaceibly to put him to Death." Lewis and Clark also told the men to go back to the Oto town and invite the Otos and Missouris to meet them at the upriver Omaha town to make peace between the Omahas and them, and any other tribes in the area.

The Corps traveled eighteen miles upstream this day.

August 8, William Clark took a walk along the riverbank with John Collins as the Corps continued upriver. Remember John? He was the one who had sampled the whiskey keg when he was supposed to be guarding it. They came upon some elk. John fired and killed his elk. Clark fired four times at his elk, but could not find him. The ever-present mosquitoes were so bad Clark wrote, "I could not keep them out of my eyes."

25

The Corps passed the mouth of the Little Sioux River in present-day Iowa and came to an island covered with uncountable pelicans. Meriwether Lewis shot and killed one. He then took detailed measurements of the pelican to the extent that he poured water into the pelican's sack and measured that it could hold five gallons.

Clark and Collins rejoined the Corps sixteen miles upriver as they made camp.

The next morning, fog detained the Corps from leaving until 7:00 a.m. They shot and killed a turkey during the day and saw lots of beaver sign. The Corps traveled seventeen miles that day. In the evening Clark wrote, "Musquetors worse this evening than ever I have Seen them." Clark wrote in his journal almost every night how bad the mosquitoes were and it seems in each journal entry they were worse than the last time.

August 10, the Corps of Discovery made over twenty-two miles this day. Clark must have been tired; he only recorded course and distance entries.

The next morning there was a hard wind followed by rain. The Corps later landed at a large hill three hundred feet high on top of which was the grave of the Omaha chief, Black Bird, who had been a strong leader who took care of his enemies by poisoning them. Black Bird died along with four hundred of his people in the 1802 smallpox epidemic. The gravesite offered a spectacular view of the surrounding countryside and the Missouri River winding through it. The Corps traveled over seventeen miles.

On August 12, the Corps of Discovery came to an area where the river was wider than usual. At 5:00 p.m., Lewis and Clark went on shore to shoot a "Prairie wolf which was barking at us as we passed." It was a coyote. They shot at it; but the coyote got away. The men saw lots of beaver and caught a very large catfish. They made twenty miles that day and spent the evening putting together packages of presents for the Omahas.

The Corps made seventeen miles on August 13, setting up camp in present-day Dakota County, Nebraska. Lewis and Clark sent Sergeant John Ordway, Pierre Cruzatte, and three other men to the Omaha town located west of the Missouri River. They took a flag and tobacco as gifts with an invitation for the Omahas to visit camp and talk.

Ordway and his men had a difficult time hiking to the town. At times, they had to break a trail through grass and thistles ten feet high. When they reached the town, they found that it was deserted. The Omahas were out buffalo hunting. It was late in the day so Ordway and the men made camp for the night about five miles from the Corps of Discovery camp. Next day, they reported to Lewis and Clark that they had found the town deserted.

August 15, Clark took ten men to a beaver dam constructed across a creek. The men made a "Brush Drag" which they pulled across the pond and caught 318 fish—"Pike, Samon, Bass, Pirch, Red horse, Small Cat, &...Silverfish." Clark also wrote he caught a shrimp but some think he meant a crayfish. He also recorded the creek had extensive beds of mussels.

Meanwhile back at camp, the men spotted a large prairie fire to the north on the east side of the Missouri River. Lewis sent Pierre Dorion, who had lived with the Yanktons, and a small party of men to investigate the fire. When they arrived at the site of the fire, they found a small group of people had made it. Whoever had made the fire had left it to burn itself out; but the fire had gotten out of control. No one was there.

On August 16, Lewis and twelve men returned to the beaver pond and used the brush drag to catch eight hundred fish. In the evening, the wind blew from the southeast cooling things down and blowing away the "Musquitors."

At 6:00 p.m., Francois Labiche, who was part of the search party, returned to camp. He told Lewis and Clark the others were following. Three Oto chiefs and their warriors, the French trader Faufon, and Moses Reed were with them. They had also caught La Liberté, but he tricked them and escaped. The Oto chiefs were willing to make peace with the Omaha through Lewis and Clark. The Corps set fire to the prairie to signal the Omaha and any other tribes who might be in the area to come to camp for a meeting.

August 18, George Drouillard and the others accompanied Moses Reed, Fuafon, the Oto chiefs and their warriors into the Corps of Discovery's camp about mid-afternoon. After a short talk with the chiefs and providing everyone a meal, Lewis and Clark tried Reed for desertion to which he confessed. They sentenced Reed to run the gauntlet four times and they would no longer consider him part of the permanent party. The permanent party were those men who were to continue on to the Pacific Ocean. The others not in the permanent party, which now included Reed, would return to St. Louis with the keelboat.

The men formed two lines facing each other. Each man held nine switches in his hands to strike Reed. When the three Oto chiefs learned what was to happen to Reed, they asked that Lewis and Clark pardon Reed; but they explained to the chiefs that it was necessary to do this to keep discipline. Reed then had to run between the two lines of men four times, as they beat him with sticks.

Lewis and Clark then met with the chiefs, Little Thief and Big Horse, and asked the reason for the war between them and the Omahas. They said two Missouris who lived with the Otos had tried to steal Omaha horses but the Omahas had killed them in the attempt, the Otos and Missouris then sought revenge and the situation escalated from there.

That evening Lewis and Clark gave everyone an extra gill of whiskey and they had a dance that lasted until 11:00 p.m.

At 10:00 a.m. on August 19, Lewis and Clark met with the Otos and Missouris. They delivered the same basic speech that they had given earlier at Council Bluffs that the government had changed to the United States, that they came in peace, and that they wanted the tribes to live in peace with their neighbors. The chiefs spoke and said they were willing to make peace with neighboring tribes, but they needed gifts to give their young men so they would keep the peace. Lewis and Clark gave peace medals to the chiefs and a paper commission to the warriors.

One warrior, Big Blue Eyes, gave his commission back, which angered Lewis and Clark. The Otos apologized then asked that Lewis and Clark give the paper back to Big Blue Eyes after he apologized. Lewis and Clark gave it to the chiefs to give to him.

At the end, the chiefs asked for a drink of whiskey which Lewis and Clark gave them. The Corps of Discovery made ready to leave; but the chiefs asked them to stay the night which they agreed to do.

Sergeant Charles Floyd became violently ill with "Beliose Cholick." All the men tried to help Floyd. The person who stayed with Floyd and attended him the most was York. York was Clark's slave. He was about the same age as Clark and had been his constant companion since childhood. Everyone was concerned for Charles Floyd's life threatening condition.

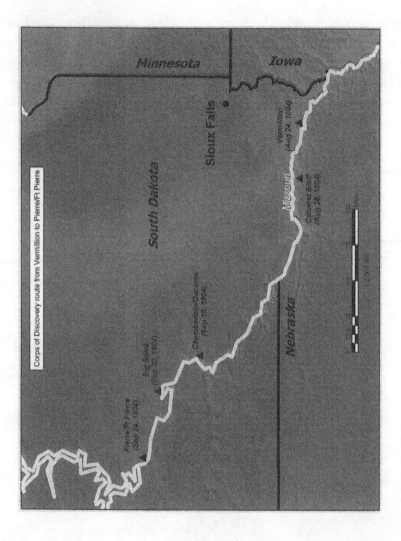

Corps of Discovery route from Vermillion to Pierre/Ft Pierre

Minnesota

Iowa

Sioux Falls

South Dakota

Vermillion
(Aug 24, 1804)

Missouri

Calumet Bluff
(Aug 28, 1804)

Chamberlain/Oacoma
(Sep 15, 1804)

Big Bend
(Sep 20, 1804)

Pierre/Ft Pierre
(Sep 24, 1804)

Nebraska

6

August 20–September 6, 1804

August 20, 1804, the Corps of Discovery was in the area of present-day Sioux City, Iowa. They had concluded a positive meeting with Oto and Missouri chiefs the day before.

Twenty-two-year-old Sergeant Charles Floyd had developed a severe case of bilious colic, violent stomach pains with severe vomiting of bile. The men cared for him through the night of August 19. Meriwether Lewis tried all the medical procedures he had been taught. William Clark, York, and others spent the night nursing Charles; but his condition only grew worse.

In the morning, Lewis and Clark gave the Otos, Missouris, and Faufon, the French trader, gifts as they rode off on their horses. The Corps of Discovery set out upriver under a gentle breeze.

Charles was no better. They pulled over to a bluff to make a warm bath for him. He said to Clark, "I am going away. I want you to write me a letter." He then died with a great deal of composure. Current thinking is he may have had appendicitis, which they could not have diagnosed or treated at that time. The Corps of Discovery buried Charles on top of what is now Floyd's Bluff with the Honors of War. Clark wrote, "This Man at all times gave us proofs of his firmness and Deturmined resolution to doe Service to his Countery and honor to himself."

A sad Corps of Discovery sailed a mile further upriver and camped on the north side of a stream they named Floyd River.

The next morning, the Corps set out early with a gentle breeze from the southeast. Approximately three miles from their camp, they passed the mouth of the Big Sioux River and were now traveling between the present-day states of Nebraska and South Dakota. They traveled more than twenty-two miles on this day.

On August 22, they stopped at a bluff that contained a variety of minerals. Lewis pounded on the rocks, smelling and tasting them. He became sick apparently poisoned by the rock. Lewis and Clark thought the rock might have contained arsenic, so Lewis took a dose of "salts" to counteract the arsenic. After traveling nineteen miles this day, Lewis and Clark held an election for sergeant to replace Charles Floyd. Patrick Gass received the majority vote.

August 23, the Corps set out early in the morning. Joe Field killed their first buffalo. Lewis and twelve men went out to drag the buffalo back to the river where they butchered it. The wind blew so hard from the west that fine sand made it hard to see and covered everything. They made ten miles this day.

It rained during the night and into the following morning. The Corps came to a bluff that people today call Ionia Volcano in Nebraska. They found the clay was so hot that they could not hold their hands to it. Apparently, a chemical reaction in the shale generates the heat.

Clark, York, and a French boy, hiked along the shore. Clark killed two buck elks, and York and the French boy each shot an elk.

The boats passed the Vermillion River on the north side of the Missouri River and made camp for the night. The French members of the expedition who had been in this area before told Lewis and Clark a strange tale about a hill today called Spirit Mound in Clay County, South Dakota. None of the local tribes would approach the mound because a tribe of spirit people lived there. These people were 18 inches tall with large heads. They had sharp arrows that could kill people at long distances. Several years ago, three Omahas had been killed by the little spirit people. Lewis and Clark decided to visit Spirit Mound.

August 25, the keelboat and one pirogue under the command of Sergeant Pryor continued upriver six miles as Lewis, Clark, ten men, and Seaman, Lewis' Newfoundland dog, set off on a hike to climb Spirit Mound about eight miles north of the Missouri River.

They left early in the morning. As the day wore on it became increasingly hot. After seven miles, Seaman gave out and Lewis sent him back to the pirogue. As the men approached Spirit Mound, a huge flock of birds swarmed around the top of the hill. By noon, the men reached the top. The birds moved off. They must have been after flying ants that now bit the men on their exposed skin. Other than that, there were no little people. From on top of the mound, they had a great view of the entire area and saw large herds of elk and buffalo.

Lewis, York, and some of the men were very tired and thirsty. They made their way to a stream and drank from a beaver pond. Later they took a forty-minute rest in a small grove. Clark found "Great quantities of the best largest grapes I ever tasted."

They reached the pirogue at sunset and set fire to the prairie to inform the Yanktons of their presence. Pryor and the rest of the Corps of Discovery further upriver saw their fire and did the same. Lewis, Clark, and the men ate supper and slept that night on a buffalo robe. They saw bats for the first time on the trip.

August 26, Lewis, Clark, and their men reached the keelboat at 9 a.m. In their absence, the horses had wandered off. Lewis and Clark left behind George Drouillard and Private George Shannon to search for the horses and then join the Corps further upriver.

Nineteen-year-old George Shannon was the youngest member of the expedition. He was born in Pennsylvania and moved with his family to Ohio in 1800. He was part of the group of nine that Clark brought with him from Kentucky. Clark did not consider him a first-rate hunter; but he did bring in his fair share of the game.

At 10 a.m., the Corps of Discovery proceeded on upriver for nine miles and made camp. Lewis and Clark formally appointed Patrick Gass as Sergeant replacing Charles Floyd.

After searching all night, Drouillard arrived in camp the next morning. He reported that he and Shannon had become separated and he could not find the horses. Lewis and Clark sent Privates John Shields and Joe Field back to look for Shannon and the horses.

The Corps continued upriver. After traveling several miles, they set the prairie on fire to let the Yanktons know that they wanted to meet with them. At 2 p.m., they reached the mouth of the James River on the north side of the Missouri River.

A boy swam from the riverbank out to one of the pirogues. The men in the pirogue paddled after him to shore where two more boys stood. The boys told the Corps that the Yanktons were camped upstream on the James River.

Lewis and Clark sent two of the boys with Sergeant Pryor, a Frenchman, and Pierre Dorion, who had been living with the Yanktons, to go to the Yankton village and invite the chiefs to a council at Calumet Bluffs further upstream on the south side of the Missouri River. The third boy who was an Omaha wanted to stay for a while with the Corps. They made fourteen miles this day.

August 28, a stiff breeze blew from the south. The river was wide, shallow, and full of sandbars. After four miles of travel, the Omaha boy left the Corps to return to the Yankton village. Clark wrote, "Capt. Lewis & my Self much indisposed—I think from the Hominy we Substitute in place of bread (or Plums)."

After over eight miles, they reached Calumet Bluff and made camp on the present-day Nebraska side of the river. Just before landing, a snag pierced a pirogue and almost sank it. The men unloaded the gear, most of which had become wet, into the other boats and got the pirogue to shore where they were able to repair it. The wind blew hard from the South.

Shields and Field caught up with the Corps. They did not find the horses or Shannon; but from the signs, it appeared Shannon had found the horses and was traveling to catch up with the Corps. The only problem was that somehow Shannon had passed the Corps without seeing them and was now upriver of them trying to catch up but only getting further ahead.

The next morning they sent John Colter after Shannon with food since Clark did not consider Shannon that good of a hunter. John was also one of the nine Kentuckians that Clark had brought to the expedition. He was born in Virginia and moved west with his family. At twenty-nine years old, John, under Drouillard's training, had become one of the Corps better hunters.

At 4 p.m., Sergeant Pryor, Dorion, the Frenchman, and seventy Yankton men arrived on the opposite shore. Lewis and Clark sent them gifts—cooking kettles, corn, and tobacco with the message that they would meet with them tomorrow.

Sergeant Pryor reported that when they first approached the village, the Yanktons wanted to carry Dorion and him on a buffalo robe into camp, an honor due a leader. They declined saying they were not the Corps leaders. The Yanktons were very hospitable, feeding Dorion and Pryor, and providing a teepee for them to stay in for the night.

The morning of August 30 started out foggy, but soon burned off. Lewis and Clark sent Dorion in a pirogue to the other side of the river to invite the Yankton chiefs and warriors for a meeting at noon. After everyone assembled, Lewis and Clark gave their speech about coming in friendship and the change in government. They gave the chiefs peace medals and the warriors commissions and other presents. They gave the principal chief a set of military clothes and an American flag. The Yankton chiefs said they needed to talk among themselves and then would respond to Lewis and Clark's speeches tomorrow. Everyone then smoked the pipe of peace. Lewis shot the air gun for everyone's entertainment.

That evening, the Yanktons formed a circle around three fires and danced late into the evening. This included recounting their deeds in battle and horse stealing raids. Dorion explained to Lewis and Clark that it was the custom to throw presents to those who danced the best. So they threw knives, tobacco, and other items to the best dancers. After the dance, the Yanktons camped alongside the Corps of Discovery that night.

The next morning after breakfast, the chiefs sat in a row each holding his pipe of peace. Shake Hand, the principal chief, spoke first. He said he was glad to hear the words of President Jefferson. He was interested in having St. Louis traders come among them. He was also interested in taking Lewis' offer to travel to Washington, D.C., to meet with the president. The other chiefs, White Crane, Struck by the Ree, and Half Man all agreed and were impressed that the Americans were more generous than the Spanish and British. After the speeches, they again smoked the pipe of peace.

Lewis and Clark asked Dorion and his sons who had been living with the Yanktons to stay with the Yanktons. They commissioned Dorion to act as the United States representative in the area. He was to attempt to make peace between the various tribes and to arrange for the principal chiefs to travel downstream to St. Louis and then on to Washington, D.C., to meet with President Jefferson. They gave Dorion an American flag, presents, and trade goods as well as a parting bottle of whiskey as he crossed to the north side of the river with the Yanktons.

September 1, the Corps of Discovery set out on a cloudy rainy day. The men were catching large amounts of catfish every day. Drouillard killed a buck elk and a beaver. They made sixteen miles upriver this day.

The Corps set out early the next morning; but only made four miles. A strong wind blew from the northwest. It was cold and rainy with thunder and lightning. They came to under a yellow bluff, which is in present-day Bon Homme County, South Dakota. They shot and killed four elk making jerky out of the meat and using the hides to cover the pirogues. The sky cleared up in the evening and the men were all in high spirits.

September 3, the Corps continued upriver another fifteen miles. They stopped at Plum Creek where they found great quantities of delicious plums. Clark liked them so much he collected seeds to send back to his brother.

They saw herds of elk and buffalo; and for the first time they saw "wild Goats…they are wild and fleet." This was their first sighting of antelope. There were now few trees. They did find signs of Colter and Shannon. It looked like Colter had not yet caught up with Shannon.

The Corps set out early on the morning of September 4, a very cold wind blew from the southeast. They made eight miles this day and camped above the mouth of the Niobrara River. Clark explored the Niobrara for about three miles and located an old abandoned Ponca town site.

The wind was blowing hard from out of the south the morning of September 5 as the Corps sailed upriver. The men saw large flocks of turkeys and grouse. They spotted more antelope on the hills, and for the first time, they saw mule deer. The Corps came to Ponca Creek in what is now Knox County, Nebraska. Lewis and Clark sent Privates John Shields and George Gibson to the Ponca town located two miles up the creek. The Poncas were not home; they were out buffalo hunting. Ironically, John and George killed a buffalo that was wandering through the town. The Corps made over thirteen miles this day.

September 6, the wind was now blowing out of the northwest after an early morning storm. The Corps made over eight miles before stopping to camp. John Colter rejoined the group. He was unable to catch up with Shannon who continued to travel rapidly upriver ahead of the Corps of Discovery.

7

September 7–23, 1804

By September 7, 1804, the Corps of Discovery had reached what is now Boyd County, Nebraska and Charles Mix County, South Dakota. George Shannon was still missing and presumed ahead of the expedition trying to catch up with it while all the time the Corps was actually behind him.

Lewis and Clark found their first prairie dog town on the Nebraska-side of the Missouri River. The men attempted to dig out a prairie dog from his burrow; but after digging down six feet and then probing further with a pole, they realized they would not be able to dig to the end of the burrow. They then tried flushing out the prairie dogs by pouring five barrels of water down a hole. They were finally able to kill one and capture another. The Corps traveled five and a half miles on this day.

September 8, Lewis shot his first buffalo. The Corps made seventeen miles upriver and was now at a point where present-day South Dakota is on both sides of the Missouri River.

The next day, the Corps came upon a herd of over five hundred buffalo. A hunting party killed several buffalo. York, a member of the party, shot his first buffalo. The Corps made fourteen miles upriver this day.

It was a dark, overcast day on September 10, as the Corps continued upriver under a gentle breeze. They came to an area now called Mulehead Point where on top of a hill they found "...a back bone with the most of the entire laying Connected for 45 feet those bones are petrified, Some teeth & ribs also Connected." They had found the remains of a plesiosaur, an aquatic dinosaur. The Corps traveled twenty miles before making camp.

The next morning, the sky was again cloudy. They passed a prairie dog town that was 800 yards wide and 970 yards long.

The Corps finally caught up with George Shannon alongside the river. He was surprised to find that he had been ahead of the expedition the whole time. He had run out of bullets early on and had lived off of one rabbit and fruit. One of the two horses had given out and was lost, so the expedition was down to one horse. The Corps made sixteen miles upriver this day.

September 12 was a dark cloudy day. The Corps had a rough go at it—passing through sandbars and shallow water. They made only eight miles this day. The men camped across the river from "a Village of Barking Prairie Squirrels."

The next day the Corps set out early. The sky was again dark with a drizzling rain. They had to pass through a number of sandbars making twelve miles before setting up camp.

The morning of September 14 was miserable with drizzling rain that lasted throughout the day. At times, the drizzle changed to hard showers. Clark killed the Corps' first antelope, and John Shields killed their first jackrabbit. Lewis described each in his journal. These were the first scientific descriptions of each animal. The Corps made nine miles this day.

On September 15, the Corps set out early. After two miles, they came to the mouth of the White River. Lewis and Clark sent Sergeant Patrick Gass and Rubin Field to explore the river for one day and then catch up with the Corps further upriver. The Corps traveled eight miles. Clark wrote, "I killed a Buck Elk & Deer, this evening is verry Cold, Great many wolves of Different Sorts howling about us. The wind is hard from the N W this evening."

The Corps broke camp at 7 a.m. the morning of September 16; but only went upriver about one and a half miles where they decided to camp by a creek for the rest of the day and the next day to dry out their supplies and equipment from all the rain the last few days. Their camping spot was near present-day Oacoma, South Dakota. Lewis and some of the hunters shot and killed several buffalo and deer. Gass and Field returned to camp after about a twelve-mile hike up the White River where they had seen level plains with great herds of buffalo and antelope.

The next day Lewis and six hunters went exploring the interior for the day. They saw wolves, hawks, skunks, and of course the ever-present prairie dogs. Herds of buffalo, elk, deer, and antelope were seen in every direction. Lewis wrote, "I do not think I exaggerate when I estimate the number of Buffaloe which could be compreed at one view to amount to 3,000." The hunters killed a buffalo and a great many deer. John Colter killed their first mule deer. The men back in camp continued to dry out the gear.

September 18, the Corps of Discovery set out early, but made only seven miles due to a hard wind blowing against them. Again, they saw lots of game and many wolves. Clark killed his first "prairie wolf" or coyote. The hunters killed ten deer this day.

The Corps continued upriver early on a cool clear morning. It was a good day; they made twenty-three miles. The hunters killed lots of game and the men on the keelboat shot two buffalo swimming across the Missouri River. Again, they saw immense herds of buffalo, elk, and antelope. The Corps made camp close to the Grand Detour of the Missouri River or Big Bend.

The morning of September 20, Lewis and Clark sent George Drouillard and John Shields with the last horse across Big Bend to the far side to hunt and jerk meat for the Corps. Clark then walked across The Narrows seeing herds of buffalo and "Goats." The boats had to navigate through many sandbars, making over thirty-three miles before camping for the night on a sandbar upriver of Big Bend.

At 1:30 a.m., the Sergeant of the Guard alerted the camp that the island they were camped on was rapidly washing away. The men quickly packed up their gear by the light of the moon and left the island. They had not reached the shore before the river's current washed away the land they had been camping on. In the morning, the Corps proceeded on upriver seeing large herds of game and making eleven miles before camping for the night.

On September 22, a thick fog detained their departure until 7 a.m. The men saw numerous herds of buffalo in every direction. After thirteen miles, they came to Cedar Island where Regis Loisel, a St. Louis trader, had built a fort to trade with the local tribes. The fort was now abandoned, but had been occupied the previous winter. The Corps of Discovery made sixteen miles this day and camped in what is now Hughes County, South Dakota.

Sunday, September 23, 1804, the Corps of Discovery set sail with a gentle breeze from the southeast. Large herds of buffalo grazed in the distance. The men saw smoke from the southwest, it must have been a local tribe setting the prairie on fire to let the Corps or others know that they were there and wished to meet. The boats had to navigate through a great many sandbars. They passed Medicine Creek and made camp for the night in present-day Hughes County across the river from Antelope Creek.

Soon after setting up camp, three Brule Lakota boys swam across the river to the camp. Through sign language and the few words that Pierre Cruzatte knew of their language, the boys said they belonged to a Brule village of sixty lodges that was camped along the next river upstream, which was the Bad River in present-day Stanley County. The boys were the ones who had set the prairie on fire to notify their village of the Corps of Discovery. Lewis and Clark gave them tobacco as presents for their chiefs and also gave them the message that Lewis and Clark wanted to talk with the chiefs the next day.

8

September 24–28, 1804

The morning of September 24 was fair, when the Corps of Discovery passed the mouth of Antelope Creek. As the Corps approached Farm Island, Lewis and Clark prepared clothes, peace medals, and other presents for the chiefs.

John Colter had been out ahead of the Corps hunting with their remaining horse. He had killed four elk and left them hanging on Farm Island for the Corps to butcher. As the keelboat passed the island, Colter ran to the bank and shouted that his horse had been stolen. Just then, five Brule men stood on the bank and wanted to get on the boat. Lewis and Clark said no. They wanted the horse back and would meet with their chiefs at the mouth of the Bad River after the horse was returned.

The Corps traveled by La Framboise Island where they saw many elk and buffalo. The boats came to off the mouth of the Bad River and anchored near present-day Fort Pierre, South Dakota.

A chief walked up to the riverbank. Clark took a pirogue over to the shore and met with him. The chief's name was Buffalo Medicine. He said his village was two miles up the Bad River. Buffalo Medicine and Clark smoked the pipe of peace. It was difficult for Cruzatte and Drouillard to communicate with Buffalo Medicine. Clark asked about the stolen horse. Buffalo Medicine said he knew nothing about it. Clark said they would meet with the chiefs and principal men tomorrow.

One-third of the men of the Corps of Discovery camped on shore for the night, the rest stayed on the keelboat. Sergeant John Ordway wrote that the five Brule men who had been on the bank caught up with them. They were very friendly and the men of the Corps invited them to eat and camp with them on shore that night which they did.

The morning of September 25 was again fair; the wind blew from the southeast. The Corps established the meeting site on a sandbar at the mouth of the Bad River. They set up a flagstaff and American flag, and also set up an awning for the chiefs to sit under.

At 11 a.m., Black Buffalo, the grand chief, and Buffalo Medicine arrived. Everyone shared food with each other. Lewis and Clark discovered that their interpreters "do not Speak the language well."

At noon, the chief, Partisan, and other important men arrived for the council. After smoking the pipe of peace, Lewis and Clark gave their speech about the United States being the new government and that they came in peace and friendship. They gave the chiefs peace medals, an American flag, knives, tobacco, and other presents. They gave Black Buffalo a red coat and a cocked hat.

After the council was concluded, Lewis and Clark invited the three chiefs and one of their principal men out to the keelboat where they showed them various instruments and equipment as well as giving each of them half a wineglass of whiskey. Partisan began to stagger about the boat. It was time for the chiefs to leave. They were reluctant to go; but Clark finally coerced them into one of the pirogues.

Clark and the pirogue's crew transported the four men to shore. As the pirogue reached the shore, three young men seized the pirogue's cable while another man hugged the mast.

Partisan told Clark the pirogue could not leave until Clark gave him and his men more presents. Clark wrote, "…his insults became So personal and his intentions evident to do me injury, I Drew my Sword (and ordered all hands under arms)." Lewis ordered all the men on the keelboat to be ready to fire their muskets and the swivel guns. The Brule all drew their bows and arrows and leveled the muskets that they had directly at Clark and his men at point blank range.

Black Buffalo stepped in to diffuse the confrontation. He took hold of the cable and ordered the three men to let go and the fourth man to let go of the mast. They obeyed and Partisan walked off twenty yards to join the rest of the men now numbering about one hundred.

Clark spoke to Black Buffalo and tried to shake his hand but he refused. Black Buffalo walked off to join the crowd of Brule men. Clark walked over to Black Buffalo and tried to shake his hand again. He also tried to shake Partisan's hand; but they both refused. All this time, men on both sides pointed arrows and musket barrels at each other. Clark walked back to the pirogue and the Corps of Discovery men began to leave the shore when Black Buffalo, Buffalo Medicine, and two principal men waded out into the river and asked to spend the night on board the boat.

Clark picked them up and took them to the keelboat. The Corps then proceeded up the river about a mile and anchored at an island they named Bad Humor Island since they "were in a bad humor."

The morning of September 26, the Corps of Discovery set out and made about four and a half miles upriver. Black Buffalo and the others asked Lewis and Clark to stop at their village so they could show their friendship. Many women and children came to the riverbank to see the keelboat. The chiefs invited Lewis and Clark to stay the night and watch their dance, which they agreed to do.

While spending time on shore, Lewis and Clark found that the Brule had captured 48 Omaha women and children. Clark advised that the Brule make peace with the Omaha and return the prisoners. Black Buffalo and Buffalo Medicine agreed to do so.

At 5 p.m., ten young men had Clark sit on a buffalo robe, then carried him to the council tents and placed him between two chiefs. They returned for Lewis and did the same thing. About 70 men sat in a circle with Lewis and Clark. They all smoked the pipe of peace, then ate supper, and smoked until dark as an elder gave a positive speech about the Corps of Discovery.

The pipes and food were cleared away, and a large fire was built. It was time for the dance. The men sang and played musical instruments while the women danced with scalps and other war trophies. The dance lasted until midnight when Lewis and Clark returned to the boats. Four chiefs joined them on the keelboat for the night.

September 27, the riverbank was lined with people come to look at the keelboat. Lewis went with the chiefs back to the village. He gave them blankets, corn, peace medals for the chiefs, and commissions for the principal men. They told Lewis that most of their people had not yet arrived and asked that the Corps stay one more night so they could meet them. Lewis agreed to do so.

Lewis, Clark, and some of the men attended the dance that evening, which was similar to the dance held the night before. At 11 p.m., Partisan and another chief went with Lewis and Clark to spend the night on the keelboat.

The keelboat was anchored out in the river. While Lewis and some of the men waited on shore, Clark and the others paddled out to the keelboat in one of the pirogues. As the pirogue reached the keelboat, it accidentally struck the keelboat's anchor cable snapping it. The keelboat rapidly drifted away with the current.

Clark shouted from the pirogue for all hands to man the oars and poles to bring the keelboat to the riverbank. Partisan thought the Omahas were attacking them and shouted a warning to the Brule that they were under attack. Hearing the commotion, Black Buffalo and two hundred men rushed to the riverbank, armed and ready for action; but soon stood down when they realized it was a false alarm.

The Corps of Discovery men pulled the keelboat up under the riverbank for the night—exposed to potential attack. Sixty Brule men camped on shore by the boat.

Later that night, Pierre Cruzatte came to Lewis and Clark and told them he had spoken with the Omaha prisoners who told him that the Brule intended to stop and rob the Corps of Discovery. The Corps remained on its guard through the night.

September 28, the Corps attempted to retrieve the lost anchor; but the shifting river sand had covered it. After breakfast, Black Buffalo requested a ride up the river to the next village.

As the Corps prepared to leave, several Brule men grabbed the keelboat's cable and held on. They wanted tobacco and Partisan wanted tobacco and a flag. After much wrangling, Lewis and Clark gave Black Buffalo tobacco to give to his men. He then jerked the cable from their grip and the keelboat headed upriver with Black Buffalo along for the ride.

Two miles upriver, they came upon Buffalo Medicine who was sitting on a sandbar. He also asked for a ride upriver which Lewis and Clark agreed to. Buffalo Medicine told them that Partisan had put the men up to holding onto the boat's cable.

A man came racing his horse full speed up to the riverbank. When he asked to come aboard the keelboat, Lewis and Clark allowed him on. He was Buffalo Medicine's son. Lewis and Clark sent him back to the Brule stating that they wanted peace; but were prepared if the Brule wanted war.

The Corps made a new anchor out of large rocks and remained anchored in the middle of the river for the night.

Over the next few days, the Corps left the chiefs off at their destinations and proceeded up the Missouri River. That winter the Corps of Discovery stayed with the Mandan Tribe in present-day North Dakota and then in the spring the Corps continued west to the Rocky Mountains and eventually on to the Pacific Ocean with a retracing of its route back to St. Louis in 1806.

Those first few months on the Missouri River tested the members of the Corps of Discovery and melded them into Clark's Band of Brothers who would be able to cross the continent and accomplish the mission President Jefferson gave them. They were to find a passage to the Pacific Ocean from the source of the Missouri River. They were to come in peace to the local inhabitants and inform them they were now part of the United States. They were to determine the prospects for trade, and take notes on local peoples and their customs. They were to take scientific observations and record anything new that they encountered. Nothing is perfect; but all in all, the Corps of Discovery accomplished its mission.

9

In The Wake Of Lewis And Clark

A yellow stick, its bark stripped by beaver, bobbed near shore in the roiling current of the Missouri River. I plucked the beaver stick from the water—a river gift to me. I stood at Three Forks, Montana, where the Jefferson, Madison, and Gallatin Rivers join forces to form the Missouri.

When Meriwether Lewis and William Clark's Corps of Discovery reached Three Forks in 1805, they had to decide which branch to take in order to proceed on in their quest for the Northwest Passage to the Pacific Ocean. Maybe you are trying to decide where to go and what to see when following Lewis and Clark's journey. In the words of Lewis and Clark, let us proceed on and look at a sample of books, maps, activities, and sites along the Lewis and Clark trail.

You may want to begin your journey of discovery by reading the journals kept by Lewis, Clark, and some of the expedition members. Nicholas Biddle edited the first journal of the expedition in 1814. Bernard DeVoto edited a one-volume edition published in 1953. Dr. Gary Moulton's recent multivolume edition with copious footnotes is a great way to delve into the expedition. Stephen Ambrose's *Undaunted Courage* is good if you do not want to wade through the journals. If you are interested in how the Native American people viewed the Corps of Discovery, then James Ronda's book *Lewis and Clark Among the Indians* is a must read. Are you interested in a modern view of Lewis and Clark's route and how it compares to Lewis and Clark's experiences? Dayton Duncan's *Out West* takes you on his own discovery of the country along Lewis and Clark's route as he travels in his Volkswagen van.

You say you do not have time to read? How about viewing Ken Burn's video "Lewis & Clark: The Journey of the Corps of Discovery." He does a great job showing the route of the expedition through photographs of the rivers, mountain passes, wildlife, and surrounding scenery.

What about maps? Besides state and AAA highway maps, there are specific maps for Lewis and Clark's trail. The National Park Service has published a good general map on the Lewis and Clark National Historic Trail. Another excellent general map is produced by the Lewis and Clark Interagency Partnership and is titled "Discovering the Legacy of Lewis and Clark." Both maps show the route of the expedition, events, landmarks, and interpretive centers.

What does the internet have to offer? Just by running a search for "Lewis and Clark", you can find 412,000 results. Two excellent websites that can take you to even more Lewis and Clark sites are Lewis and Clark Trail Heritage Foundation at http://www.lewisandclark.org/index.htm and The National Lewis and Clark Bicentennial Council at www.lewisandclark200.org. There is even a site http://www.esri.com/lewisandclark/interactive_maps.html that has an interactive map and a virtual tour of the country the expedition passed through. As with any internet site, these site addresses may change over time.

There are many trails, parks, and sites to visit. A few of these are: Katy Trail State Park in Missouri, Sergeant Floyd Monument and Interpretive Center in Iowa, Spirit Mound, the Narrows, and Wakpa Sica (Bad River) Reconciliation Place in South Dakota, Ft. Mandan and the Lewis and Clark Interpretive Center in North Dakota, Gates of the Mountains and Traveler's Rest State Park in Montana, Lolo Trail National Historic Landmark, Nez Perce National Historic Park in Idaho, Cape Disappointment in Washington, and Ft. Clatsop National Memorial in Oregon.

One final way to experience what Lewis and Clark experienced is to find a stretch of river or a mountain trail the Corps of Discovery traveled and spend time there alone or with a small group. One such place is on the Upper Missouri National Wild and Scenic River in Montana. This portion of the river flows 150 miles from Ft. Benton to Robinson Bridge in the Charles M. Russell National Wildlife Reserve. The only way to see this stretch of river is by water. The scenery is little changed since the Corps of Discovery passed through that region.

What better way to experience the Lewis and Clark country than to sit by a campfire after a good day's paddle on the river, finishing off a hearty supper. The black night sky spangled with its myriad of stars, coyotes howl on a distant ridge, as tall tales, laughter, and camaraderie abound. A night like that just might give a fleeting taste of what the Corps of Discovery experienced as you follow in the wake of Lewis and Clark.

Bibliography

Ambrose, Stephen E. *Undaunted Courage, Meriwether Lewis, Thomas Jefferson, and the Opening of the American West*, Simon & Schuster, New York, New York, 1996.

Biddle, Nicholas. *The Journals of the Expedition Under the Command of Captains Lewis and Clark*, The Heritage Press Edition, Norwalk, Connecticut, 1993.

Christian, Shirley, *Before Lewis and Clark, The Story of the Chouteaus, the French Dynasty That Ruled America's Frontier*, Farrar, Straus and Giroux, New York, New York, 2004.

DeVoto, Bernard. *The Journals of Lewis and Clark*, Houghton Mifflin Company, Boston, Massachusetts, 1953.

Jones, Landon Y. *William Clark and the Shaping of the West*, Farrar, Straus and Giroux, New York, New York, 2004.

Kukla, Jon. *A Wilderness So Immense, The Louisiana Purchase and the Destiny of America*, Alfred A. Knopf, New York, New York, 2003.

Moulton, Gary E. *The Definitive Journals of Lewis & Clark, From the Ohio to the Vermillion*, Volume 2 of the Nebraska Edition, University of Nebraska Press, Lincoln, Nebraska, 1986.

Moulton, Gary E. *The Definitive Journals of Lewis & Clark, Up the Missouri to Fort Mandan*, Volume 3 of the Nebraska Edition, University of Nebraska Press, Lincoln, Nebraska, 1987.

Moulton, Gary E. *The Definitive Journals of Lewis & Clark, John Ordway and Charles Floyd*, Volume 9 of the Nebraska Edition, University of Nebraska Press, Lincoln, Nebraska, 1995.

Moulton, Gary E. *The Definitive Journals of Lewis & Clark, Patrick Gass*, Volume 10 of the Nebraska Edition, University of Nebraska Press, Lincoln, Nebraska, 1996.

Moulton, Gary E. *The Definitive Journals of Lewis & Clark, Joseph Whitehouse*, Volume 11 of the Nebraska Edition, University of Nebraska Press, Lincoln, Nebraska, 1997.

Ronda, James P. *Lewis and Clark Among the Indians*, University of Nebraska Press, Lincoln, Nebraska, 1984.

Schuler, Harold H. *Lewis & Clark in the Pierre and Fort Pierre Area*, Pierre Convention & Tourism Bureau, Pierre Chamber of Commerce and Harold H. Schuler, Pierre, South Dakota, 2001.

Smith, Page. *The Shaping of America, A People's History of the Young Republic*, Volume III, McGraw-Hill Book Company, New York, New York, 1980.

About The Author

Bill Markley was born on St. Patrick's Day in 1951. He and his wife Liz have been married twenty-five years and have two children, Becky and Christopher. Bill is active in church, as a Boy Scout leader, and is a member of the Encounters on the Prairie Executive Board, the local chapter of the Lewis and Clark Trail Heritage Foundation. Bill works for the South Dakota Department of Environment and Natural Resources as the Ground Water Quality Program Administrator.

While on annual leave from his job, Bill had the good fortune to be an extra in five movies including *Dances With Wolves*, *Son of the Morning Star*, *Far and Away*, *Gettysburg*, and *Crazy Horse*. He was a member of an Antarctic research team for two expeditions in 1972 and 1973 in the Dry Valleys of Antarctica. As a boy, he worked on the family farm in Pennsylvania taking care of cattle, horses, and other animals as well as general farm work. He has a BS degree in Biology and an MS degree in Environmental Science and Engineering from Virginia Polytechnic Institute and State University. His favorite hobbies include writing, reading, Civil War infantry and frontier cavalry reenacting, hiking, and camping.

Bill has lived in Fairview Village, Pennsylvania, for 17 years, Blacksburg, Virginia, for 6 years, and Pierre, South Dakota, for 29 years. He has kayaked and backpacked in Alaska, traveled to Hawaii, the Bahamas, Canada, Antarctica, New Zealand, Fiji, the Kingdom of Tonga, and spent a week on the Pacific Ocean traveling from Tonga to New Zealand aboard a Tongan banana boat. Bill has kept journals through most of his experiences, possibly material for future books. Bill has written magazine and newspaper articles and *Dakota Epic Experiences of a Reenactor During the Filming of Dances With Wolves*. He is currently a member of the Western Writers of America. Go to www.billmarkley.com for more information on Bill and his writing.

978-0-595-37272-0
0-595-37272-4

CPSIA information can be obtained
at www.ICGtesting.com
Printed in the USA
LVHW111618290721
693757LV00006B/103

9 780595 372720